Financial Literacy for teenagers and young adults Simplified

Learn How to Invest, Control, and Save Money to Create a Safe and Successful Future

Profitable Man

Table of Contents

INTRODUCTION...3

CHAPTER ONE 7

Assessing Your Financial Situation: The Crucial Role of an Emergency Fund 7

Assessing Your Financial Situation: The Art of Managing Income and Debt Repayments Effectively..11

Establishing Healthy Money Habits: A Roadmap to Financial Security 16

CHAPTER TWO 21

Establishing Healthy Money Habits: Crafting a Personalized Budget for Financial Well-being...21

Smart Financial Choices in Education: Exploring Alternatives to Student Loans 26

Smart Financial Choices in Education: Making Informed Decisions about Educational Investments 32

CHAPTER THREE..37

Building Wealth through Investments: Making Money Work for You with Passive Income Strategies 37

Building Wealth through Investments: Transforming Bad Debt into Good Debt for Sustainable Prosperity 41

Building Wealth through Investments: Navigating the World of Cryptocurrency with Essential Investment Principles.......................46

CHAPTER FOUR 51

Building Wealth through Investments: Avoiding Common Pitfalls to Safeguard Your Savings...51

Legal and Strategic Financial Planning: Effectively Reducing Tax Bills 57

CHAPTER FIVE 62

Legal and Strategic Financial Planning: The Advantages of Entrepreneurship and Creating Multiple Income Streams 62

Legal and Strategic Financial Planning: Strategies for Maintaining Financial Stability Even in the Face of Job Loss...................................68

A Holistic Approach to Long-Term Financial Security: Legal and Strategic Financial Planning 74

CONCLUSION 80

Navigating the Financial Landscape of Young Adulthood

Embarking on the journey into adulthood brings with it a wave of newfound independence, opportunities, and responsibilities. Yet, the financial challenges that accompany this phase of life can be particularly daunting for young adults. From managing student loans and credit card debt to contemplating retirement savings, the financial landscape can seem complex and overwhelming. This is where the significance of developing a positive money mindset becomes paramount.

Understanding the Financial Challenges Faced by Young Adults:

Young adults often find themselves at the crossroads of financial vulnerability. The desire for independence, coupled with the temptation to acquire material possessions, can lead to overspending and accumulating debt. Many individuals in this age group are just starting their careers, which may not yield substantial incomes, making it challenging to save or invest. The burden of student loans further compounds the situation, and the looming specter of retirement planning often takes a back seat in the face of immediate financial concerns.

The transition from adolescence to adulthood involves critical decisions about education, career paths, and lifestyle choices, all of which have profound implications on one's financial well-being. Unfortunately, the lack of financial education in traditional educational curricula leaves many young adults ill-equipped to navigate these challenges successfully. As a result, they may find themselves ensnared in a cycle of debt and financial uncertainty.

Importance of Developing a Positive Money Mindset:

A positive money mindset is the cornerstone of financial success. It involves cultivating a healthy relationship with money, understanding its role as a tool for achieving goals, and embracing responsible financial habits. Developing this mindset empowers young adults to take control of their finances, make informed decisions, and build a foundation for long-term financial security.

A positive money mindset goes beyond merely budgeting or saving; it involves adopting a proactive and intentional approach to financial choices. It encourages individuals to view money not as a source of stress but as a means to create opportunities and fulfill aspirations. By instilling confidence and financial literacy, a positive money mindset equips young adults to face challenges, weather economic uncertainties, and make prudent decisions that align with their long-term objectives.

Overview of the Guide's Objective: Achieving Financial Security through Simplified Strategies:

The purpose of this guide is to demystify the intricacies of personal finance for young adults and provide practical, actionable strategies for achieving financial security. Through simplified approaches and clear insights, the guide aims to empower readers with the knowledge and tools necessary to make informed financial decisions.

The guide is designed to address common financial pitfalls faced by young adults, offering guidance on building emergency funds, navigating student loans, creating effective budgets, and making smart investment choices. It emphasizes the importance of developing a positive money mindset as the foundation for financial success. By the end of the journey through these pages, readers will not only have a clearer understanding of their financial situation but also possess the skills and mindset needed to navigate the path to financial security with confidence and resilience.

CHAPTER ONE

Assessing Your Financial Situation: The Crucial Role of an Emergency Fund

Financial stability is the bedrock upon which a secure and independent future is built. One of the key pillars of this stability is the often-underestimated emergency fund. Assessing your financial situation begins with understanding the critical importance of having a robust emergency fund and knowing how to build one.

Understanding the Significance of an Emergency Fund:

Life is unpredictable, and financial emergencies can strike at any moment. Whether it's unexpected medical expenses, car repairs, or sudden job loss, having a financial safety net can mean the difference between temporary setbacks and long-term financial turmoil. An emergency fund serves as a buffer, providing a sense of financial security and preventing individuals from falling into the debt trap when unforeseen circumstances arise.

The primary purpose of an emergency fund is to cover essential living expenses during times of crisis without resorting to high-interest loans or credit cards. It acts as a financial cushion, allowing individuals to navigate unexpected challenges with resilience and minimal disruption to their overall financial well-being. Without this safety net, individuals may find themselves facing difficult choices, compromising their financial stability in the process.

How to Build an Emergency Fund:

Building an emergency fund requires a deliberate and disciplined approach. Here are key steps to consider:

Set a Realistic Goal: Determine how much you want to save in your emergency fund, typically aiming for three to six months' worth of living expenses. This amount should cover essential costs like rent or mortgage, utilities, groceries, and insurance.

Create a Budget: Assess your monthly income and expenses to identify areas where you can cut back and allocate funds towards your emergency fund. Creating a budget helps prioritize saving and ensures that you consistently contribute to your fund.

Automate Savings: Set up automatic transfers to your emergency fund each month. Treating savings like a non-negotiable expense ensures a consistent and gradual buildup of funds over time.

Separate Accounts: Consider keeping your emergency fund in a separate account to prevent easy access for non-emergencies. This separation helps maintain the fund's integrity and discourages impulsive spending.

Adjust as Needed: Life circumstances change, and so should your emergency fund goals. Reassess your financial situation regularly and adjust your savings goals accordingly.

Prioritize High-Interest Debt: Before fully funding your emergency fund, consider paying down high-interest debts. This ensures that you're not simultaneously accumulating debt while trying to build a financial safety net.

In conclusion, assessing your financial situation involves recognizing the pivotal role of an emergency fund. It's not just about preparing for the unexpected; it's about proactively safeguarding your financial stability. By understanding the significance of an emergency fund and following a strategic approach to build one, you take a significant step toward achieving financial resilience and independence.

Assessing Your Financial Situation: The Art of Managing Income and Debt Repayments Effectively

Understanding your financial situation requires a meticulous examination of both your income streams and debt obligations. This holistic approach ensures a comprehensive overview, allowing individuals to make informed decisions, create sustainable budgets, and work towards financial stability. In this exploration, we delve into the crucial aspects of evaluating monthly income and managing debt repayments effectively.

Evaluating Monthly Income:

The foundation of financial assessment lies in a clear understanding of your monthly income. This includes not only your primary job salary but also any additional sources of income such as freelance work, part-time jobs, or side hustles. To assess your financial situation accurately, it's essential to consider the net income—the amount you take home after deductions for taxes and other withholdings.

Determine Your Total Income: Compile all sources of income to calculate your total monthly earnings. This provides a realistic view of the funds available for budgeting and debt management.

Consider Variable Income: If your income fluctuates due to factors like commission-based work or irregular hours, consider an average monthly income to create a more stable financial plan.

Account for Windfalls: Include any irregular income such as bonuses, tax refunds, or gifts in your assessment. While these are not guaranteed, factoring them in can provide additional financial flexibility.

Managing Debt Repayments Effectively:

Debt can be a significant impediment to financial well-being, but managing it strategically is key to achieving stability. Effectively handling debt repayments involves a combination of understanding your outstanding balances, prioritizing repayments, and seeking opportunities to reduce interest payments.

Compile a List of Debts: Create a comprehensive list of all outstanding debts, including credit cards, student loans, and any other liabilities. Note the interest rates and minimum monthly payments for each.

Prioritize High-Interest Debts: Devote extra attention to high-interest debts, as they can accumulate quickly. Prioritize paying off these debts first to minimize the long-term financial impact.

Explore Consolidation Options: Investigate the possibility of consolidating multiple debts into a single, more manageable payment with a lower interest rate. This can simplify repayments and potentially reduce overall interest costs.

Negotiate Terms with Creditors: In cases of financial hardship, don't hesitate to reach out to creditors. Many are willing to negotiate terms or create repayment plans that better align with your current financial situation.

Allocate a Percentage of Income to Debt Repayment: Establish a dedicated portion of your monthly income for debt repayment. This systematic approach ensures consistent progress in reducing outstanding balances.

Avoid Accumulating New Debt: While repaying existing debt, make a conscious effort to avoid accumulating new debt. This requires discipline in managing expenses within the limits of your income.

In conclusion, assessing your financial situation involves a careful examination of both income and debt. By understanding the nuances of your monthly income and implementing effective strategies for debt repayment, you pave the way for financial stability. This process requires diligence and a proactive approach, but the long-term benefits of achieving debt-free status and enhanced financial well-being make it a worthwhile endeavor.

Establishing Healthy Money Habits: A Roadmap to Financial Security

In the pursuit of financial security, the significance of cultivating healthy money habits cannot be overstated. These habits serve as the building blocks of a stable and prosperous financial future, providing a framework for responsible financial management. In this exploration, we delve into the identification and adoption of ten key money habits that are instrumental in achieving and maintaining financial security.

1. Budgeting with Purpose:

Establishing a budget is not merely about tracking expenses; it's about allocating resources purposefully. Begin by categorizing spending, distinguishing between needs and wants, and setting realistic limits for each category. Regularly review and adjust your budget to align with changing financial goals and circumstances.

2. Prioritizing Savings:

Cultivate the habit of paying yourself first by allocating a portion of your income to savings before addressing other expenses. Whether it's contributing to an emergency fund, retirement account, or other savings goals, consistent saving builds a financial cushion that enhances your overall financial security.

3. Avoiding Impulse Spending:

Impulse spending can derail even the most thoughtfully crafted budget. Develop the discipline to differentiate between immediate desires and long-term goals. Implement strategies such as creating shopping lists, practicing delayed gratification, and avoiding unnecessary purchases to curb impulsive spending.

4. Regularly Reviewing Financial Statements:

Stay actively engaged with your financial statements, including bank statements, credit card statements, and investment accounts. Regular reviews help identify discrepancies, track spending patterns, and ensure that you are well-informed about your financial standing.

5. Investing for the Future:

Embrace the power of compound interest by making strategic investments. Whether it's in stocks, bonds, or retirement accounts, start early and stay consistent. The habit of investing builds wealth over time, contributing significantly to long-term financial security.

6. Limiting Debt Accumulation:

Adopt a cautious approach towards debt, focusing on responsible borrowing and timely repayments. Prioritize paying off high-interest debts, avoid accumulating unnecessary debt, and use credit wisely to maintain a healthy financial profile.

7. Emergency Fund Maintenance:

Building an emergency fund is not a one-time task; it requires ongoing maintenance. Regularly assess your emergency fund's adequacy based on current living expenses and make adjustments as needed to ensure it remains a robust safety net during unexpected financial challenges.

8. Continuous Financial Education:

Stay informed about financial trends, investment opportunities, and changes in economic landscapes. Commit to lifelong learning about personal finance, empowering yourself to make informed decisions that align with your financial goals.

9. Negotiating and Seeking Value:

Develop the habit of seeking value in your financial transactions. Whether negotiating bills, exploring discounts, or shopping strategically, actively look for opportunities to maximize the value of your money.

10. Setting and Reassessing Financial Goals:

- Establish clear and achievable financial goals, whether short-term or long-term. Regularly reassess these goals, celebrate milestones, and adjust them to align with evolving life circumstances. Goal-setting provides direction and motivation for maintaining healthy money habits.

In conclusion, establishing healthy money habits is a transformative journey toward financial security. These ten key habits, when adopted and ingrained into daily financial practices, serve as a roadmap for building resilience, achieving goals, and ensuring a stable and prosperous financial future. By fostering these habits, individuals empower themselves to navigate the complexities of personal finance with confidence and purpose.

CHAPTER TWO

Establishing Healthy Money Habits: Crafting a Personalized Budget for Financial Well-being

At the heart of financial stability lies the art of budgeting – a skill that not only allows individuals to manage their expenses but also serves as a powerful tool for wealth creation. Building a custom budget that aligns with personal goals is a cornerstone of establishing healthy money habits. In this exploration, we delve into the intricacies of crafting a personalized budget that not only meets immediate needs but also lays the foundation for long-term financial success.

Understanding the Significance of Budgeting:

Budgeting is not merely about restricting spending; rather, it's a proactive and strategic approach to managing finances. A well-crafted budget serves as a roadmap, providing a clear picture of income, expenses, and savings goals. By understanding where money is coming from and where it's going, individuals gain control over their financial narrative, fostering financial security and peace of mind.

Steps to Build a Custom Budget:

Define Financial Goals: Before diving into the nitty-gritty of budgeting, it's essential to identify short-term and long-term financial goals. Whether it's saving for a home, paying off debt, or building an emergency fund, these objectives will shape the structure of your budget.

Gather Income Information: Compile a comprehensive list of all sources of income. This includes salary, bonuses, freelance income, and any other inflows. Accurate income information forms the foundation of your budget.

List Monthly Expenses: Categorize and list all monthly expenses, including fixed costs like rent or mortgage, utilities, groceries, transportation, and discretionary spending on entertainment and dining out.

Distinguish Between Needs and Wants: Differentiate between essential needs and discretionary wants. While needs are non-negotiable, wants can be adjusted based on financial goals and priorities.

Allocate for Savings and Investments: A crucial aspect of budgeting is allocating a portion of your income to savings and investments. Prioritize contributions to an emergency fund, retirement accounts, and other investment vehicles.

Create Realistic Categories: Customize your budget categories based on your lifestyle and spending patterns. This customization ensures that your budget is a practical reflection of your financial reality.

Factor in Irregular Expenses: Consider irregular expenses such as annual insurance premiums, holiday spending, or medical costs. Allocate funds each month to a dedicated category to cover these irregular but expected costs.

Track and Adjust: Regularly monitor your spending against your budget. This not only helps in identifying areas for improvement but also allows for adjustments to accommodate changing circumstances or priorities.

Emergency Fund Contribution: Include a line item for contributions to your emergency fund. Building and maintaining this financial safety net is a critical component of a robust budget.

Review and Revise Periodically: Life is dynamic, and so should be your budget. Regularly review your financial goals, income, and expenses. Adjust your budget to align with changing priorities and circumstances.

Aligning Budget with Wealth Creation:

A well-crafted budget isn't just about managing day-to-day expenses; it's a powerful tool for wealth creation. By consistently saving and investing a portion of your income, you position yourself to achieve long-term financial goals such as homeownership, retirement, and financial independence.

In conclusion, building a custom budget that aligns with personal goals is a fundamental step towards establishing healthy money habits. It empowers individuals to take control of their financial destiny, prioritize what matters most to them, and work towards a future of financial security and abundance. It's not about restricting oneself but about making intentional choices that contribute to both immediate well-being and long-term prosperity.

Smart Financial Choices in Education: Exploring Alternatives to Student Loans

Education is a powerful investment in one's future, but the rising costs of tuition and associated expenses often lead many students to rely on student loans. However, a thoughtful and strategic approach to financing education can mitigate the burden of student loans. In this exploration, we delve into alternatives to student loans that not only offer financial relief but also contribute to smart financial choices in education.

1. Scholarships and Grants:

Scholarships and grants provide an excellent way to fund education without incurring debt. Many organizations, institutions, and foundations offer financial assistance based on academic achievement, extracurricular activities, or specific skills. Students are encouraged to actively seek out and apply for these opportunities, tapping into a valuable resource for funding that doesn't require repayment.

2. Work-Study Programs:

Participating in work-study programs allows students to gain work experience while financing their education. These programs, often offered by universities, provide part-time employment opportunities on or off-campus, aligning with students' academic schedules. Earnings from work-study can contribute to tuition and living expenses, helping students avoid accumulating debt.

3. Community College and Transfer Programs:

Starting education at a community college before transferring to a four-year institution is a cost-effective strategy. Community colleges generally have lower tuition rates, allowing students to complete foundational coursework at a more affordable cost before transitioning to a larger institution for specialized studies. This approach minimizes the need for extensive loans.

4. Employer Tuition Assistance:

Some employers offer tuition assistance programs as part of their employee benefits. This valuable resource can significantly reduce the financial burden of education. By combining work and education, individuals can enhance their skills while having a portion or all of their tuition covered by their employer.

5. Income-Share Agreements (ISAs):

ISAs are emerging as an innovative alternative to traditional student loans. In an ISA arrangement, investors fund a student's education, and, in return, the student agrees to share a percentage of their future income for a specified period. This model aligns the financial interests of investors with the success of the student, providing a unique avenue for funding education without immediate debt obligations.

6. Online Learning and MOOCs:

Leveraging online learning platforms and Massive Open Online Courses (MOOCs) can be a cost-effective way to acquire skills and knowledge. Many MOOCs offer courses from renowned institutions at a fraction of the cost of traditional education. This approach allows individuals to pursue education at their own pace and often without the need for student loans.

7. Apprenticeships and Vocational Training:

For those seeking hands-on skills and a direct entry into the workforce, apprenticeships and vocational training programs are valuable alternatives. These programs provide practical, job-focused education with minimal or no tuition costs, allowing individuals to earn while they learn and avoid the financial strain of student loans.

8. Military Service and ROTC Programs:

Joining the military or participating in Reserve Officers' Training Corps (ROTC) programs can provide financial assistance for education. Service members may be eligible for tuition assistance, the GI Bill, or other military education benefits, significantly reducing or eliminating the need for student loans.

9. Crowdfunding and Educational Savings:

Crowdfunding platforms and educational savings accounts offer additional avenues for financing education. Friends, family, and even strangers may contribute to a student's educational fund through crowdfunding, while dedicated savings accounts allow individuals to systematically save for education over time.

10. Dual Enrollment Programs:

High school students can explore dual enrollment programs, enabling them to earn college credits while still in high school. This accelerates the path to a degree and can lead to substantial cost savings on tuition. By strategically planning coursework, students can reduce the overall financial burden of higher education.

In conclusion, smart financial choices in education involve exploring diverse alternatives to student loans. By adopting a proactive and strategic approach, individuals can access quality education while minimizing the financial impact. These alternatives not only alleviate the pressure of immediate debt but also contribute to a more financially secure future.

Smart Financial Choices in Education: Making Informed Decisions about Educational Investments

Education is undoubtedly one of the most significant investments a person can make, shaping not only career paths but also influencing financial outcomes. In the realm of smart financial choices in education, the focus extends beyond just the acquisition of knowledge; it encompasses strategic decisions that consider long-term financial implications. This exploration delves into the importance of making informed decisions about educational investments, ensuring that the pursuit of knowledge aligns with financial goals.

Understanding Educational Investments:

Educational investments go beyond the traditional view of tuition fees; they encompass a broader spectrum, including costs related to tuition, books, living expenses, and potential lost income during the study period. Viewing education as an investment underscores the need to assess the return on investment (ROI) in terms of career opportunities and earning potential.

Research Program ROI: Before committing to a particular program, research the expected return on investment. Consider factors such as the average salary for graduates, employment rates, and industry demand for the chosen field.

Explore Financial Aid Options: Investigate scholarships, grants, and other forms of financial aid that can significantly reduce the overall cost of education. These options can lighten the financial burden and contribute to a more favorable ROI.

Consider Community College or Trade Schools: Traditional four-year universities are not the only path to success. Community colleges and trade schools often provide specialized, cost-effective education that leads to high-demand careers.

Evaluate Online and Part-Time Programs: Online and part-time programs offer flexibility and can be more affordable than traditional full-time options. These alternatives enable individuals to work while pursuing education, minimizing the impact on income.

Making Informed Decisions:

Informed decision-making involves a thorough evaluation of potential educational investments, weighing the costs against the expected benefits. It requires a strategic approach to aligning educational choices with personal and financial goals.

Assess Individual Financial Capacity: Understand your current financial situation and evaluate how much you can realistically afford to invest in education. Consider creating a budget that includes tuition, living expenses, and potential lost income.

Factor in Opportunity Cost: Recognize that pursuing education often involves a temporary sacrifice of income. Factor in the opportunity cost of not working during study years and assess whether the long-term benefits justify the short-term financial trade-off.

Explore Employer-sponsored Education: Some employers offer education benefits or tuition reimbursement programs. Investigate whether your current or potential employer provides such opportunities, reducing the financial burden on your end.

Seek Professional Guidance: Consult with career counselors, financial advisors, or individuals in your desired field to gain insights into the value of specific educational investments. Their experiences and perspectives can provide valuable guidance in making informed decisions.

In conclusion, making informed decisions about educational investments is a pivotal aspect of smart financial choices in education. By understanding the broader concept of educational investments, researching potential programs, and aligning choices with personal and financial goals, individuals can ensure that their pursuit of knowledge becomes a strategic investment in their future financial success.

CHAPTER THREE

Building Wealth through Investments: Making Money Work for You with Passive Income Strategies

In the pursuit of financial security and independence, mastering the art of making money work for you is paramount. Beyond the realm of traditional employment, the concept of passive income and strategic investment becomes a cornerstone for building lasting wealth. This exploration delves into the significance of making money work for you through passive income and investment strategies.

Understanding Passive Income:

Passive income is income earned with little to no direct effort. Unlike the active income derived from a traditional job, passive income streams continue to generate money even when you're not actively working. This concept opens the door to financial freedom by allowing individuals to accumulate wealth and enjoy financial security without being bound to a nine-to-five job.

Diversifying Income Streams: Passive income often arises from various sources, including investments, real estate, royalties, and dividends. Diversifying income streams helps mitigate risk and ensures a more resilient financial portfolio.

Real Estate Investments: Real estate is a classic avenue for passive income. Rental properties, real estate crowdfunding, or Real Estate Investment Trusts (REITs) can provide steady cash flow and potential appreciation over time.

Investing in Dividend Stocks: Dividend-paying stocks allow investors to earn a share of a company's profits regularly. This not only provides a steady income stream but also offers the potential for capital appreciation.

Creating and Selling Intellectual Property: Authors, musicians, and content creators can generate passive income through royalties from books, music, or other intellectual property. Once created, these assets can continue to generate income over time.

Strategic Investment Approaches:

Investment strategies play a crucial role in making money work for you. Strategic decisions, coupled with a long-term perspective, can amplify returns and contribute significantly to wealth accumulation.

Long-Term Investing: Adopting a long-term investment approach helps ride out market volatility and capitalizes on the power of compounding. Consistent contributions to investment accounts over time can lead to substantial wealth growth.

Risk Management: Assessing risk tolerance and diversifying investments are fundamental to successful wealth-building. Balancing high-risk, high-reward assets with more stable options helps create a resilient investment portfolio.

Automated Investing: Utilize automated investment platforms or robo-advisors to streamline the investment process. These tools can help maintain a disciplined investment approach, ensuring consistent contributions and portfolio rebalancing.

Educate Yourself: Informed decision-making is crucial in the world of investments. Continuously educate yourself about different asset classes, market trends, and investment strategies to make informed choices that align with your financial goals.

By integrating passive income streams and strategic investment approaches, individuals can position themselves for financial success. The goal is not just wealth accumulation but the creation of a financial ecosystem that provides ongoing, sustainable income. Making money work for you through passive income and strategic investments lays the foundation for long-term financial independence and the realization of life goals.

Building Wealth through Investments: Transforming Bad Debt into Good Debt for Sustainable Prosperity

Debt, often perceived as a financial burden, can be a double-edged sword. While bad debt can hinder financial progress, strategic planning and financial literacy can turn it into a powerful tool for wealth creation. This exploration delves into the concept of transforming bad debt into good debt, showcasing how savvy financial decisions can propel individuals toward sustainable prosperity through intelligent investment strategies.

Understanding Bad Debt and Good Debt:

Bad Debt:

Bad debt typically refers to high-interest, non-productive liabilities that do not contribute to asset creation or income generation. Examples include credit card debt, payday loans, or other forms of consumer debt that accrue interest at rates that can impede financial stability.

Good Debt:

Good debt, on the other hand, is debt used to acquire assets or investments that have the potential to appreciate in value or generate income. Examples include mortgage loans for real estate, student loans for education, or business loans for entrepreneurial ventures. Good debt is seen as an investment in one's future financial well-being.

Strategies for Transforming Bad Debt into Good Debt:

Consolidation and Refinancing: One effective strategy is to consolidate high-interest debts into a single, lower-interest loan. This reduces the overall interest burden, making the debt more manageable and freeing up resources for wealth-building activities.

Educational Investments: Consider leveraging debt for education that enhances employability and earning potential. Student loans, when used judiciously, can be considered good debt if they contribute to increased future income and career opportunities.

Real Estate Investment: Using debt to finance real estate acquisitions is a common way to transform bad debt into good debt. The potential for property appreciation and rental income can offset the initial debt, leading to long-term wealth accumulation.

Entrepreneurial Ventures: Taking on debt to fund a business venture can be a strategic move, provided the business has a solid plan for profitability. Many successful entrepreneurs have utilized loans to start or expand businesses, turning the borrowed capital into a lucrative investment.

Investing in Marketable Skills: Borrowing to acquire skills and certifications that enhance professional qualifications can be a wise move. This positions individuals for better career opportunities, higher income, and, ultimately, a positive return on the debt investment.

Risk Management and Financial Discipline:

While transforming bad debt into good debt holds potential, it's crucial to approach this strategy with careful consideration and financial discipline.

Risk Assessment: Evaluate the potential risks and returns associated with the investment. Ensure that the expected benefits outweigh the costs, including interest payments.

Budgeting and Planning: Integrate debt repayment plans into a comprehensive budget. Prioritize high-interest debts and allocate funds strategically to ensure timely repayment.

Emergency Fund: Maintain an emergency fund to cover unexpected expenses and provide a financial buffer in case of unforeseen challenges.

Continuous Learning: Stay informed about personal finance, investment strategies, and market trends. Continuous learning empowers individuals to make informed decisions and adapt to changing financial landscapes.

In conclusion, transforming bad debt into good debt is a nuanced process that requires thoughtful planning, risk assessment, and financial discipline. When approached strategically, leveraging debt for wealth creation can pave the way for long-term prosperity and financial independence. This shift in perspective underscores the transformative potential of debt when used as a tool for intelligent investment rather than a mere financial burden.

Building Wealth through Investments: Navigating the World of Cryptocurrency with Essential Investment Principles

In the dynamic landscape of wealth creation, the emergence of cryptocurrency has added a new dimension to investment opportunities. Navigating the world of cryptocurrency requires a nuanced understanding of this digital asset class and the application of essential investment principles. This exploration delves into the intricacies of investing in cryptocurrencies, emphasizing key principles for building wealth in this evolving and sometimes volatile market.

Understanding Cryptocurrency:

Cryptocurrency, led by Bitcoin and a multitude of altcoins, represents a decentralized form of digital currency based on blockchain technology. Unlike traditional currencies issued and regulated by governments, cryptocurrencies operate on a decentralized network, offering potential advantages such as increased security, transparency, and financial inclusivity.

Educate Yourself: Cryptocurrency markets can be complex, and understanding the technology, market dynamics, and potential risks is paramount. Take the time to educate yourself about blockchain, how cryptocurrencies work, and the different projects and tokens available in the market.

Diversification in Cryptocurrencies: Like traditional investments, diversification is a key principle in cryptocurrency investing. While Bitcoin is often considered a flagship cryptocurrency, exploring other projects (altcoins) can provide a more diversified portfolio, spreading risk and potentially enhancing returns.

Risk Management: Cryptocurrency markets are known for their volatility. Implementing sound risk management strategies, such as setting stop-loss orders and not investing more than you can afford to lose, helps mitigate the inherent risks associated with this asset class.

Essential Investment Principles:

Building wealth through cryptocurrency investments involves applying fundamental investment principles that are integral to any asset class.

Long-Term Perspective: Cryptocurrency markets can experience short-term volatility, but adopting a long-term perspective can help weather these fluctuations. Consider the underlying technology, utility, and long-term potential of the projects in which you invest.

Stay Informed: Cryptocurrency markets evolve rapidly, influenced by technological developments, regulatory changes, and market sentiment. Staying informed about industry news, market trends, and potential catalysts can help you make informed investment decisions.

Security and Storage: Given the digital nature of cryptocurrencies, securing your holdings is crucial. Use reputable wallets, employ secure practices such as two-factor authentication, and consider hardware wallets for long-term storage.

Due Diligence: Conduct thorough research before investing in any cryptocurrency. Understand the project's whitepaper, team, community support, and potential use cases. Due diligence is critical to identifying projects with long-term viability.

Regulatory Awareness: Cryptocurrency markets are subject to evolving regulatory landscapes. Stay aware of regulatory developments in your jurisdiction and globally, as regulatory changes can significantly impact the market.

In conclusion, navigating the world of cryptocurrency with essential investment principles requires a combination of education, strategic planning, and a disciplined approach. While the potential for wealth creation in this space is substantial, it comes with inherent risks. By applying fundamental investment principles and staying informed, individuals can harness the opportunities presented by cryptocurrency markets, contributing to a diversified and resilient wealth-building strategy.

CHAPTER FOUR

Building Wealth through Investments: Avoiding Common Pitfalls to Safeguard Your Savings

Investing is a powerful tool for wealth creation, but it comes with inherent risks. Navigating the financial markets successfully requires not only sound strategies but also a keen awareness of potential pitfalls. This exploration delves into common investment mistakes to avoid, providing insights into safeguarding your savings and building a robust investment portfolio.

1. Lack of Diversification:

Mistake: Overconcentration in a single asset or asset class exposes investors to heightened risk. If that particular investment performs poorly, the entire portfolio may suffer.

Avoidance Strategy: Embrace diversification by spreading investments across different asset classes, industries, and geographic regions. A well-diversified portfolio can help mitigate the impact of underperforming assets.

2. Emotional Decision-Making:

Mistake: Allowing emotions to drive investment decisions, such as panic selling during market downturns or euphoric buying during rallies, can lead to suboptimal outcomes.

Avoidance Strategy: Develop a disciplined investment strategy and stick to it. Regularly review and rebalance your portfolio based on your predetermined goals and risk tolerance, minimizing the influence of short-term market fluctuations.

3. Ignoring Risk Management:

Mistake: Neglecting risk management strategies, such as setting stop-loss orders or having an exit plan, can expose investments to significant losses.

Avoidance Strategy: Implement risk management tools to protect your investments. Set realistic profit and loss targets, diversify your portfolio, and consider using stop-loss orders to limit potential losses.

4. Chasing Performance:

Mistake: Investing based solely on recent strong performance may lead to buying assets at their peak, with subsequent underperformance.

Avoidance Strategy: Focus on the long-term fundamentals of an investment rather than short-term performance. Avoid chasing trends and conduct thorough research before making investment decisions.

5. Neglecting Due Diligence:

Mistake: Investing in assets without proper research or understanding can result in unexpected risks and poor performance.

Avoidance Strategy: Conduct thorough due diligence before making any investment.

Understand the fundamentals, risks, and potential returns of the assets in your portfolio. Stay informed about market trends and economic indicators.

6. Timing the Market:

Mistake: Attempting to predict market movements and time the buying and selling of assets is challenging and often leads to missed opportunities or losses.

Avoidance Strategy: Instead of trying to time the market, adopt a systematic approach such as dollar-cost averaging. Invest regularly, regardless of market fluctuations, to benefit from the natural ebb and flow of asset prices over time.

7. Failing to Reassess and Adjust:

Mistake: Neglecting to periodically reassess your investment strategy in light of changing market conditions, personal financial goals, or life circumstances can hinder long-term success.

Avoidance Strategy: Regularly review your investment portfolio, considering changes in your financial situation, risk tolerance, and market conditions. Adjust your strategy accordingly to ensure alignment with your evolving objectives.

In conclusion, avoiding common investment mistakes is crucial for safeguarding your savings and building lasting wealth. By embracing diversification, managing emotions, conducting thorough research, and maintaining a disciplined approach, investors can navigate the complexities of financial markets with resilience and confidence. Continuous learning and adaptation contribute to a robust investment strategy that stands the test of time.

In the realm of legal and strategic financial planning, one of the paramount considerations is the effective reduction of tax bills. As individuals strive to build wealth and secure their financial futures, understanding and implementing legal means to minimize tax liabilities becomes a crucial component of a comprehensive financial strategy. This exploration delves into the importance of reducing tax bills, the legal avenues available, and strategic financial planning to optimize tax efficiency.

The Significance of Reducing Tax Bills:

Taxes represent a significant portion of an individual's financial responsibilities, and minimizing this burden is essential for wealth creation. Reducing tax bills not only preserves more of your hard-earned income but also provides additional resources that can be strategically deployed for investments, savings, or other financial goals. Legal and ethical tax planning is a fundamental aspect of financial responsibility, ensuring compliance with regulations while optimizing tax efficiency.

Understanding Tax Structures: Different types of income and assets are subject to various tax structures. Understanding the distinctions between ordinary income, capital gains, and dividends is crucial for implementing effective tax planning strategies.

Maximizing Deductions and Credits: Leveraging deductions and credits is a key aspect of reducing tax bills. Deductions, such as those related to mortgage interest, charitable contributions, and education expenses, can significantly lower taxable income. Additionally, taking advantage of tax credits, such as those for education or energy-efficient home improvements, directly reduces the amount of taxes owed.

Strategic Retirement Contributions: Contributing to retirement accounts, such as 401(k)s or IRAs, not only helps secure financial futures but also offers immediate tax benefits. Contributions to these accounts are often tax-deductible, reducing taxable income for the year.

Optimizing Investment Strategies: Implementing tax-efficient investment strategies can minimize the tax impact of capital gains and dividends. Techniques such as tax-loss harvesting and holding investments for the long term can contribute to lower tax liabilities.

Utilizing Tax-Advantaged Accounts: Taking advantage of tax-advantaged accounts, such as Health Savings Accounts (HSAs) or Flexible Spending Accounts (FSAs), provides an avenue for tax-free contributions and withdrawals when used for qualified medical expenses.

Strategies for Legal and Strategic Financial Planning:

Regularly Reviewing Tax Laws: Tax laws are subject to change, and staying abreast of these changes is essential for effective tax planning. Regular reviews with financial advisors or tax professionals can help ensure that strategies align with current regulations.

Seeking Professional Guidance: Consulting with tax professionals or financial advisors can provide personalized insights into optimizing tax efficiency based on individual financial situations. Professionals can identify opportunities, navigate complex tax codes, and ensure compliance with legal requirements.

Year-Round Tax Planning: Instead of waiting until tax season, implementing a year-round tax planning approach allows for proactive decision-making. Regular assessments of income, expenses, and potential tax-saving opportunities contribute to a more strategic and efficient tax plan.

Considering Estate Planning: Estate planning is an integral part of legal and strategic financial planning. Properly structured estate plans can minimize estate taxes and ensure a smooth transfer of assets to beneficiaries.

In conclusion, effectively reducing tax bills through legal means is not only a financial responsibility but also a strategic approach to wealth creation. By understanding tax structures, maximizing deductions and credits, and implementing tax-efficient strategies, individuals can optimize their financial positions. Seeking professional guidance, staying informed about tax laws, and adopting a proactive year-round approach contribute to a robust legal and strategic financial plan that safeguards savings and fosters long-term financial success.

CHAPTER FIVE

Legal and Strategic Financial Planning: The Advantages of Entrepreneurship and Creating Multiple Income Streams

In the realm of legal and strategic financial planning, the pursuit of entrepreneurship and the creation of multiple income streams stand out as powerful strategies for building wealth and achieving financial security. This exploration delves into the myriad advantages of entrepreneurship and the strategic diversification of income, emphasizing how these endeavors contribute to a robust and resilient financial plan.

Entrepreneurship as a Financial Catalyst:

Unlimited Income Potential: One of the primary advantages of entrepreneurship is the potential for unlimited income. Unlike traditional employment, where income is often capped by salary structures, entrepreneurs have the opportunity to scale their businesses, resulting in uncapped earning potential.

Control Over Financial Destiny: Entrepreneurs have the autonomy to shape their financial destinies. By building and managing their businesses, they can make strategic decisions that directly impact profitability and overall financial success.

Tax Benefits: Entrepreneurship often comes with unique tax advantages. Business expenses, deductions related to business activities, and opportunities to structure income more tax-efficiently contribute to a more favorable tax position.

Asset Creation and Appreciation: Successful entrepreneurship involves the creation and growth of assets. Whether it's a thriving business, intellectual property, or valuable brand equity, these assets can appreciate over time, contributing to long-term wealth.

Innovative Wealth-Building Strategies: Entrepreneurs can leverage innovative strategies to build wealth. This may involve creating and selling products, developing passive income streams, or adopting unique business models that generate revenue even when not actively working.

Creating Multiple Income Streams for Financial Resilience:

Diversification Against Risk: Relying on a single source of income, such as a traditional job, exposes individuals to significant risk in the event of job loss or economic downturns. Creating multiple income streams acts as a hedge against these risks, ensuring financial resilience.

Passive Income Generation: Diversifying income streams allows for the creation of passive income. Whether through investments, real estate, or other ventures, passive income provides ongoing financial support with less day-to-day involvement.

Flexibility and Adaptability: Multiple income streams provide individuals with greater flexibility and adaptability. In a rapidly changing economic landscape, having diverse sources of income allows for agility in responding to market shifts or personal life changes.

Opportunities for Skill Monetization: Individuals possess a range of skills that can be monetized beyond their primary profession. Whether it's freelancing, consulting, or teaching, these skills can become additional income streams.

Strategic Risk Management: Creating multiple income streams is a strategic form of risk management. If one source of income faces challenges, the impact on overall financial stability is mitigated by alternative revenue sources.

Strategies for Entrepreneurship and Multiple Income Streams:

Identify Niche Opportunities: Entrepreneurial success often lies in identifying niche opportunities and addressing specific needs. This requires market research and a keen understanding of consumer demands.

Invest in Skill Development: Developing a diverse skill set enhances the potential for creating multiple income streams. Acquiring skills relevant to different industries or markets expands opportunities for income generation.

Leverage Technology: Technology has democratized entrepreneurship and income generation. Online platforms, e-commerce, and digital marketing offer accessible avenues for creating and scaling businesses.

Build a Financial Safety Net: While pursuing entrepreneurship and multiple income streams, it's essential to build a financial safety net. This ensures a buffer during the initial phases of business development or when transitioning to new income streams.

Seek Professional Guidance: Entrepreneurship and diversified income strategies benefit from professional guidance. Consulting with financial advisors, legal experts, and business mentors provides valuable insights and ensures compliance with legal and financial regulations.

In conclusion, entrepreneurship and the creation of multiple income streams play pivotal roles in legal and strategic financial planning. These endeavors offer the advantages of unlimited income potential, control over financial destiny, and innovative wealth-building opportunities. Simultaneously, diversifying income sources provides financial resilience, flexibility, and strategic risk management. By embracing entrepreneurship and cultivating diverse income streams, individuals can construct a financial framework that not only safeguards against uncertainties but also propels them towards enduring financial success.

Legal and Strategic Financial Planning: Strategies for Maintaining Financial Stability Even in the Face of Job Loss

In the dynamic landscape of personal finance, the prospect of job loss can be a challenging and unsettling reality. However, through strategic financial planning and legal considerations, individuals can proactively implement strategies to maintain financial stability even in the face of unforeseen employment changes. This exploration delves into the importance of preparing for job loss, legal safeguards, and strategic financial planning to weather such uncertainties.

Understanding the Importance of Financial Stability Amid Job Loss:

Job loss can have significant financial implications, affecting income, benefits, and overall financial well-being. While it may be impossible to predict or prevent job loss entirely, proactive planning ensures that individuals are better equipped to navigate these challenges and maintain financial stability during periods of unemployment.

Emergency Fund Preparation: Building and maintaining an emergency fund is a fundamental aspect of financial planning. This fund serves as a financial safety net, covering essential living expenses during periods of job loss, reducing reliance on credit cards or loans.

Legal Safeguards and Severance Packages: Understanding employment contracts, severance packages, and legal rights is crucial. Consulting with legal professionals can provide insights into entitlements, including severance pay, unemployment benefits, and potential legal recourse if job loss is wrongful or unjust.

Reviewing and Updating Insurance Policies: Adequate insurance coverage, including health, life, and disability insurance, is essential. Reviewing and updating insurance policies during employment ensures that individuals have necessary coverage, mitigating financial risks associated with unforeseen events.

Strategic Financial Planning Strategies:

Budgeting and Expense Management: Creating a detailed budget and cutting non-essential expenses can help stretch available funds during periods of unemployment. Prioritizing essential expenses, such as housing, utilities, and groceries, ensures that limited resources are allocated wisely.

Exploring Multiple Income Streams: Diversifying income sources, such as through part-time work, freelancing, or creating passive income streams, provides additional financial support. Multiple income streams offer resilience during job loss and contribute to overall financial stability.

Debt Management and Negotiation: Assessing and managing existing debt is crucial. Communicating with creditors, negotiating interest rates or payment plans, and exploring debt consolidation options can alleviate financial strain and create more manageable repayment schedules.

Career Development and Skill Enhancement: Continuously investing in career development and acquiring new skills enhances employability. This strategic approach not only improves prospects for reemployment but also positions individuals for career advancements and increased earning potential.

Utilizing Unemployment Benefits Wisely: If eligible for unemployment benefits, using these resources judiciously is crucial. Creating a budget that incorporates these benefits and aligns with financial priorities ensures that unemployment support is maximized.

Networking and Professional Relationships: Maintaining a robust professional network can facilitate job opportunities and career advice during periods of unemployment. Building and nurturing professional relationships contribute to long-term career resilience.

Legal Considerations:

Understanding Employment Contracts: Familiarizing oneself with employment contracts and agreements ensures awareness of any contractual obligations, rights, and potential compensation in the event of job loss.

Non-Compete and Non-Disclosure Agreements: Understanding the implications of non-compete and non-disclosure agreements is crucial. Legal advice can help individuals navigate these contracts and explore opportunities without violating legal constraints.

Seeking Legal Advice for Wrongful Termination: If job loss is perceived as wrongful or unjust, seeking legal advice is essential. Professionals can assess the situation, determine potential legal recourse, and guide individuals through the process of addressing unfair employment practices.

In conclusion, strategies for maintaining financial stability during job loss involve a combination of legal awareness and strategic financial planning. By preparing for the unexpected, understanding legal safeguards, and implementing proactive financial strategies, individuals can weather the challenges of unemployment and emerge with financial resilience. The key lies in cultivating a holistic approach that combines legal knowledge with strategic financial foresight, creating a robust foundation for long-term financial stability.

A Holistic Approach to Long-Term Financial Security: Legal and Strategic Financial Planning

In the pursuit of long-term financial security, a holistic approach to legal and strategic financial planning is indispensable. This comprehensive strategy goes beyond merely accumulating wealth; it involves thoughtful consideration of legal frameworks, strategic financial decisions, and a mindset that anticipates and navigates the complexities of the financial landscape. This exploration delves into the facets of a holistic approach, emphasizing the integration of legal and strategic financial planning for sustained financial well-being.

Understanding Holistic Financial Security:

Holistic financial security encompasses more than just amassing wealth; it involves a multifaceted approach that considers legal frameworks, risk management, and strategic financial decisions. This comprehensive perspective ensures that individuals not only accumulate wealth but also protect and grow it over the long term.

Legal Foundations: A holistic financial plan begins with a solid legal foundation. This includes essential documents such as wills, trusts, and powers of attorney. Establishing these legal structures ensures that one's wishes are honored and assets are protected, contributing to long-term financial security.

Insurance Strategies: Risk mitigation is a crucial element of a holistic financial plan. Adequate insurance coverage, including life insurance, health insurance, and property insurance, safeguards against unforeseen events, providing a financial safety net in times of need.

Strategic Investment and Diversification: Building long-term financial security involves strategic investment decisions. Diversifying investments across different asset classes helps mitigate risk and enhance the potential for returns. Regular assessments and adjustments to the investment portfolio align it with evolving financial goals.

Debt Management: Holistic financial planning involves a proactive approach to debt management. This includes minimizing high-interest debt, strategically using low-interest debt for wealth-building purposes, and having a systematic plan for debt repayment.

Emergency Fund and Liquidity: Maintaining an emergency fund is a cornerstone of financial security. This fund acts as a buffer against unexpected expenses or income disruptions. Ensuring liquidity in the financial portfolio provides flexibility and the ability to seize opportunities or weather economic downturns.

Strategies for Maintaining Financial Stability:

Continuous Learning and Adaptability: The financial landscape is dynamic, and a commitment to continuous learning is essential. Staying informed about economic trends, investment opportunities, and changes in tax laws enables individuals to adapt their financial strategies accordingly.

Professional Guidance: Engaging with financial advisors, tax professionals, and legal experts is instrumental in crafting a holistic financial plan. Professionals provide insights, identify potential risks, and offer guidance on optimizing financial decisions within legal frameworks.

Budgeting and Lifestyle Choices: A holistic approach to financial security involves conscientious budgeting and mindful lifestyle choices. Regularly reviewing and adjusting spending habits ensures that financial goals align with one's evolving priorities.

Social Security and Retirement Planning: Incorporating social security benefits and strategic retirement planning into the financial strategy ensures a secure and comfortable retirement. Proactive retirement planning includes contributions to retirement accounts, such as 401(k)s and IRAs.

Multiple Income Streams: Creating multiple income streams, such as entrepreneurship, investments, or side hustles, enhances financial resilience. Diversifying income sources provides a buffer against job loss or economic uncertainties.

In conclusion, a holistic approach to long-term financial security requires the integration of legal and strategic financial planning. Establishing legal foundations, managing risks, and making informed financial decisions contribute to a robust financial plan that can withstand the test of time. By continuously adapting to changing circumstances, seeking professional guidance, and embracing a diversified approach, individuals can forge a path towards enduring financial well-being.

Nurturing Financial Well-being for a Secure
Future

In the intricate web of legal and strategic financial
planning, the journey towards long-term financial
security demands a holistic approach. As we
culminate this exploration, it is imperative to

revisit key principles and strategies, instill encouragement for developing financial discipline, and underscore the attainability of financial security through the right mindset and actions.

Recap of Key Principles and Strategies:

Throughout this comprehensive guide, we have unraveled a multitude of financial principles and strategies. From understanding the importance of emergency funds to exploring the world of cryptocurrency, each segment has contributed to a comprehensive framework for building financial resilience. Assessing income, managing debt effectively, and making informed decisions about educational investments are foundational steps. Diversifying income streams, investing wisely, and reducing tax bills underscore the strategic aspects of wealth creation. The advantages of entrepreneurship, creating multiple income streams, and maintaining financial stability in the face of job loss highlight the importance of adaptability and foresight. A holistic approach has been emphasized, incorporating legal means, strategic planning, and a mindset conducive to long-term financial success.

Encouragement for Developing Financial Discipline:

Developing financial discipline is both an art and a skill. It requires a commitment to long-term goals, the ability to make informed decisions, and resilience in the face of financial challenges. As individuals embark on the journey towards financial discipline, it's essential to acknowledge that the path may not always be linear. Setbacks may occur, but it is in overcoming these hurdles that true financial discipline is forged. Embrace the learning process, seek knowledge continuously, and remain open to adapting strategies as circumstances evolve.

The encouragement for financial discipline is rooted in the understanding that discipline is the bridge between financial goals and their realization. It involves cultivating healthy money habits, consistently saving and investing, and making intentional choices that align with overarching financial objectives. Remember, discipline is not about deprivation; rather, it is about making choices that contribute to sustainable financial well-being.

Emphasizing the Attainability of Financial Security:

As we conclude, it is crucial to dispel the notion that financial security is an unattainable ideal. The right mindset and actions can pave the way for a secure and independent future. Warren Buffett aptly remarked, "The most important investment you can make is in yourself." This sentiment underscores the significance of continuous self-improvement, financial education, and cultivating a positive money mindset.

Financial security is not a distant destination but a journey that unfolds with intentional steps and informed decisions. It is within reach for individuals who are committed to their financial well-being, who embrace the principles outlined in this guide, and who recognize that every small action contributes to the larger tapestry of financial security.

In conclusion, the journey towards financial security is multifaceted, encompassing various elements of income management, investment strategies, and disciplined decision-making. As individuals internalize these principles, develop financial discipline, and maintain a positive mindset, they embark on a trajectory that leads not only to financial security but also to a life enriched by the possibilities that come with it. The empowerment to control one's financial destiny lies within the grasp of those who are willing to embark on this transformative journey.